Taking care of someone as they approach the end of their life is different than taking care of someone who is going to get better. Most people don't know that.

This booklet is a guide for keeping people comfortable at the end of their life. It provides basic insights into discomfort as the end of life approaches and explains the role of medications.

There are only two ways to die: fast or gradually. Fast death is getting hit by a truck, a heart attack, a stroke, suicide. A person is alive one minute and dead the next.

Gradual death occurs from old age or a disease that is not fixable. Dying from old age or disease has a process to it. It doesn't just happen. That process takes years for old age and months for disease. Gradual death is not painful. The disease that is causing death is what causes pain. Not all diseases that people die from cause pain.

Pain Scale

How a person expresses pain, talks about pain, and displays pain is based not on the severity of the physical pain but on their personality. To use an example: A stoic person will tend to down play their pain while a very sensitive person may think a hang nail is a level 7 on the pain scale.

The pain scale is a measurement tool used to gauge how much pain a person is experiencing. How bad is the pain? The number 10 is the worst pain and 0 is no pain. 10-9-8-7-6-5-4-3-2-1-0. Knowing what number the pain is NOW helps us understand a person's comfort level which determines what type and how much pain medicine to give.

Dying Is Not Painful. Disease Causes Pain.

When assessing for pain at the end of life the first thing we do is look at the person's disease history. Some diseases that we die from cause no pain. If that is the case then just because the person is actively dying does not mean that now they are in pain.

The signs of labor (1 to 3 weeks before death) can be interpreted as painful but in reality the labor to die is not painful. As death approaches the body feels tired, heavy, and flu like. Ibuprofen or Acetaminophen are appropriate to address the discomfort.

If there is a disease history of pain (there are a lot of painful diseases that result in death) then just because a person is dying does not mean the pain has stopped. In fact, the pain often becomes harder to manage.

As gradual death approaches nothing in the body works the way it should. Medication is not going to work in a normal time frame and the normal amount is not going to get circulated throughout the body.

Fear

We are all going to be afraid to some degree when it comes time to die. When a physician says "I can't fix you," fear immediately becomes part of our life (whether we acknowledge it or not). Fear makes physical pain hurt more.

To offer comprehensive pain management we have to look at all factors of the person, not just the physical disease. That said, we must beware of categorizing people. Pain is pain no matter how severe or minimal it is presented. The healthcare professional's job in pain management is to provide comfort and use as many methods as they can find to reach that goal. How each person deals with discomfort becomes their level of pain. It is not up to us to decide what hurts or how much pain is pain.

Standardized Dosages

There is no quick solution to effective pain management. Because everyone's pain threshold and pain level is different each individual's dosage has to be discovered, and that takes time.

There is no standardized dosage for end of life pain medicine. If I have a headache two aspirins will make it go away and probably will make it go away for most people. That is what a standardized dose is, one size fits all.

One size does not fit all in end of life pain management. Finding the right dosage of pain medicine depends upon where the person is in the process of dying. Does the healthcare professional have months to work with a person or days? That makes a big difference.

If pain has been part of the disease process then hopefully there is already a pain management protocol in place before the actual dying process has begun.

As death approaches we now address the pain that has been part of the disease process differently. We may have to increase the dosage to achieve comfort. During this time we observe, adjust, observe some more and maybe adjust again until comfort is reached. It requires time. Remember, there isn't a one dose fits all approach to end of life pain management.

Sleeping and being non-responsive (does not respond to what is happening around them) are not signs that comfort has been reached. Body language is our guide. That said, there will come a time during the labor that a person will become non-responsive, not from the medication but as part of the normal dying process.

Around the Clock

Give pain medicine around the clock, 24/7. Pain medication doesn't make the pain go away. It simply covers it up. Whatever in the body is causing discomfort is still present. As the medication wears off, the pain is again present. This is why it is important to give any kind of pain medication around the clock, to keep the medication in the blood stream, to keep the "cover" on the pain.

Overdosing

Signs of an overdose from a narcotic begin with confusion, then hallucination, then sleep, then slowed breathing, and then breathing stops. There are a lot of signs that tell us "too much" which allow us time to withhold the next dose. Then the following doses are adjusted down.

Addiction

At end of life addiction is not an issue. BUT addiction can be an issue when a narcotic consistently exceeds the amount of pain in a *healthy* person's body. If the medication equals the amount of pain in anyone's body there is no addiction.

Restlessness

Agitation, restlessness, random hand movements, sleeping with eyes partially open, muttering, or talking but not making sense are all part of the labor of dying AND are not painful. Severe agitation can be treated with anti-anxiety or antipsychotic drugs.

Levels of Pain Medicine

There are varying levels of pain medications. Low pain is treated with anti-inflammatory drugs, often non prescription, over-the-counter. Moderate to severe pain is treated with opioid analgesics, including morphine and fentanyl. Sadly, the line between moderate and severe pain treatment is often blurred.

Misconception: Morphine Kills

I think morphine and all the drugs that contain morphine are the most feared and least understood of all the pain medications.

The example I am going to use occurs way too often (This does not apply to a healthy person with no disease): A person is in the labor of dying. They are given morphine and 20 minutes or even an hour later they die. The family now believes that the morphine killed their loved one.

Here is why the morphine wasn't the cause of death: When a person is that close to death the circulation is not working normally so the medication does not have time to get to the heart and lungs where it causes death.

A normal body takes 30 to 40 minutes for medications, given by mouth, to begin to have an effect. As a person is dying from old age or disease their body is not functioning normally so it will take even longer for the medication to begin working---if it will work at all.

Shortness Of Breath

A little bit of morphine given for shortness of breath can be very helpful.

Laxative

Anyone taking pain medicines on a regular basis should be taking a laxative along with it, even when the person is in the labor of dying. If you think the person has only days before death, then you can stop the laxative. BUT remember labor can be weeks and we do not want someone going through the discomfort of weeks without a bowel movement.

Pain Management In The Last Days

Pain management is different in the last few days of life. The person is sleeping with their eyes partially open, often restless, blood pressure is dropping, pulse increasing, breathing getting slower. The person is probably non-responsive. At this point they are not going to be able to tell us if they are in pain.

First, we look at what their disease is and what their disease history has been. Was pain a part of their history? If it was, hopefully they have already been taking some form of pain medicine. If it is oral and they can no longer swallow on command, get an equivalent dosage in liquid and place it under their tongue. Also, anything you can give by mouth you can insert into the rectum.

There is generally no need to resort to IV medications or injections when a person can't swallow. IV medications combined with fluid can increase the fluid in the lungs, add to congestion, and actually make a person more uncomfortable.

Observe the person. Do they appear unduly agitated? If they are a danger to themselves in their agitation then an anti-anxiety or antipsychotic drug would be appropriate with the pain medicine.

If pain has not been part of this person's disease process then they are probably not in pain now. Observe how restless they are. Does body language indicate there is an area that is more uncomfortable than any other? Is there moaning? These may be indicators that for whatever reason now this person is in pain.

If you determine there is pain even though there is no disease history of pain that doesn't mean you have to jump right into a narcotic. Maybe a low to moderate pain medication will bring comfort. Narcotics should not be our first line of pain management anywhere in the disease process. That said, there are always exceptions.

In end of life care we just can't make one size fits all statements. We have to observe and make decisions on each person, their disease, and how they are responding and reacting to their disease.

Supplemental Comfort

Any supplemental comfort therapies we can use are always helpful. In the months before death anything that relaxes can enhance the medicine and even create a situation where less medication is needed.

Music, massage, meditation, hypnosis, and Reiki, all have a place in the months before death. In the weeks to hours before death music, Reiki, and massage can produce relaxation. Again, the key to getting out of our body is to relax, so anything that helps relaxation is beneficial.

Sleep To Relieve Pain

There is no reason with today's medical knowledge for anyone to die in pain.

For intolerable end of life pain, sometimes the only recourse to having tried everything with no success is to medicate to the point of sedation. I consider this a last resort but it is a direction to consider if the disease pain is intolerable as the end of life approaches.

Before doing this you need to have an in-depth conversation with everyone involved in the person's care about "sleeping" through the unmanageable, intolerable pain (operative words here are intolerable and unmanageable). Everyone must be on the same page in understanding the comfort goal. This is not about hastening death. This is an option for providing relief from intolerable pain until death comes naturally.

Again, there is no *quick* solution to effective pain management at the end of life. Everyone's pain threshold and pain level is different.

Your first line of resource on pain management is

your hospice nurse, or if you are not using hospice then talk with your physician. Talk about end of life pain management, ask what the physician's plan is for keeping your loved one comfortable. There are no unimportant or stupid questions.

My booklets, *Gone From My Sight* and *The Eleventh Hour* are written specifically for end of life education. *Gone From My Sight* gives the signs of approaching death. *The Eleventh Hour* offers a guide to what we can do while death is approaching.

Pain creates a box that traps us inside. The box keeps us from seeing, hearing, reacting. Hurt and discomfort and me is all the box can hold. There isn't room for anything else.

Summary of Guidelines

- The pain scale is a measurement tool used to gauge how much pain a person is experiencing. The number 10 is the worst pain and 0 is no pain. 10-9-8-7-6-5-4-3-2-1-0.

- How each person deals with discomfort becomes their level of pain.

- Dying is not painful. Disease causes pain.

- Look at the person's disease history to see if pain is part of the disease.

- Because everyone's pain threshold and pain level is different you have to adjust the dosages and that takes time.

- Give pain medicine around the clock, 24/7.

- There are a lot of signs that tell us "too much" medication and allows us time to withhold the next dose.

- Restlessness is part of the natural dying process.

- There are levels of pain medications: low pain; moderate pain; severe pain.

- Always take a laxative with moderate or severe pain medicine.

- Pain management is different in the last few days of life.

- Any supplemental comfort therapies are always helpful.

BARBARA KARNES RN
end of life education materials

www.bkbooks.com • bkbooks@bkbooks.com

ORDER FORM

CONTACT NAME: _____

ORGANIZATION: _____

STREET: _____

CITY: _____ STATE: _____ ZIP: _____

PHONE: _____ FAX _____

EMAIL: _____

❏ NEW ORDER   ❏ REORDER   PO# : _____

BILLING ADDRESS: (IF DIFFERENT FROM ABOVE)

BILLING CONTACT / ORGANIZATION: _____

STREET: _____

CITY: _____ STATE: _____ ZIP: _____

PAYMENT:

❏ INVOICE US (AGENCIES ONLY - Net 30 days)

❏ CHECK ENCLOSED (Payable to B. Karnes Books)

❏ CREDIT CARD (enter card information below)

NAME ON CARD: _____

CREDIT CARD #: [_____] [_____] [_____] [_____]

EXP DATE: _____ CVV CODE:_____

Barbara Karnes Books
MAIL TO: PO Box 822139 • Vancouver, WA 98682
Phone (9-4 pm PST) 360-828-7132 • Fax 360-828-7142

PRODUCT TITLE (See Catalog)	LANGUAGE	QTY	$ PER UNIT (See Chart Below)	SUBTOTAL

TOTAL	$
POSTAGE (See Chart Below)	$
SALES TAX (We Collect for Only These States: GA, IL, IN, KS, MI, MN, NC, OH, VA and WA)	$
GRAND TOTAL FOR ORDER (add together Total, Postage, Sales Tax)	$

Pricing & Discounts for Booklets
1 – 9	$3.00 per copy
10 - 99	$2.00 per copy
100 – 249	$1.80 per copy
250 - 499	$1.70 per copy
500 - 999	$1.60 per copy
1,000 - 2,499	$1.50 per copy
2,500 - 4,999	$1.40 per copy
5,000 - 9,999	$1.30 per copy
10,000 - 24,999	$1.20 per copy

Call for Priority Shipping rates. Quantity discounts are applied to individual products. Postage may be adjusted for rate increases. Visit **www.bkbooks.com** for discounts, postage rates not listed, secure credit card orders, new materials, and eBooks. All fees are subject to change without notice.

Postage & Handling
1 copy	$3.00
2 copies	$4.00
3 – 9 copies	$5.00
10 – 25 copies	$6.00
26 – 50 copies	$8.00
51 – 100 copies	$10.00
101 – 250 copies	$18.00
251 – 300 copies	$25.00
301 – 500 copies	$35.00

Barbara Karnes Books
MAIL TO: PO Box 822139 • Vancouver, WA 98682
Phone (9-4 pm PST) 360-828-7132 • Fax 360-828-7142